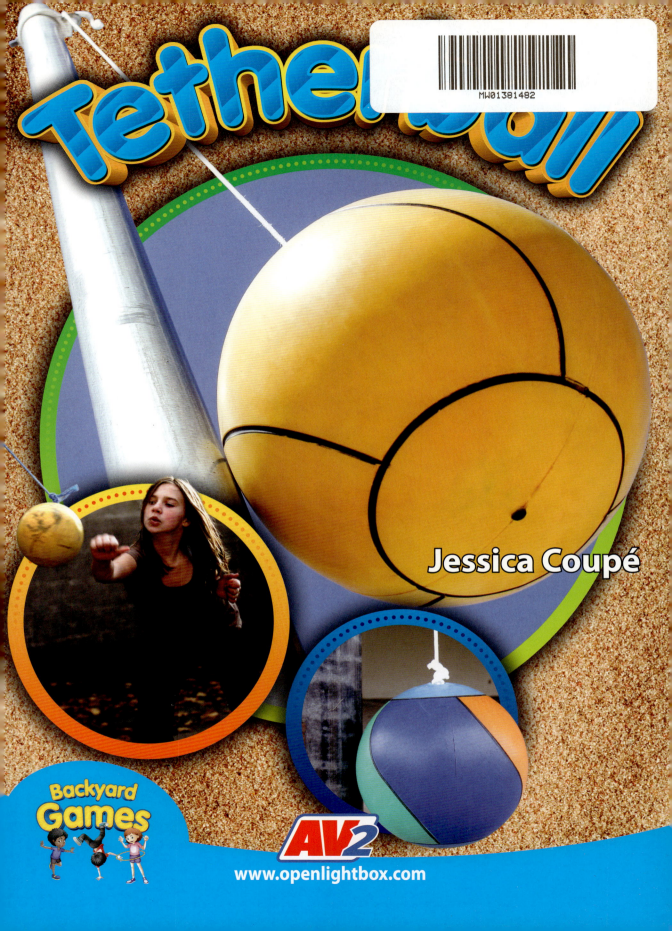

Step 1
Go to www.openlightbox.com

Step 2
Enter this unique code

HZPQE8VYG

Step 3
Explore your interactive eBook!

AV2 is optimized for use on any device

Your interactive eBook comes with...

Contents
Browse a live contents page to easily navigate through resources

Audio
Listen to sections of the book read aloud

Videos
Watch informative video clips

Weblinks
Gain additional information for research

Slideshows
View images and captions

Try This!
Complete activities and hands-on experiments

Key Words
Study vocabulary, and complete a matching word activity

Quizzes
Test your knowledge

Share
Share titles within your Learning Management System (LMS) or Library Circulation System

Citation
Create bibliographical references following the Chicago Manual of Style

This title is part of our AV2 digital subscription

1-Year 3–8 Subscription
ISBN 978-1-7911-3306-1

Access hundreds of AV2 titles with our digital subscription.
Sign up for a FREE trial at www.openlightbox.com/trial

Tetherball

CONTENTS

AV2 Book Code 2
What Is Tetherball? 4
Timeline 6
What You Need 8
The Court 10
Rules of the Game 12
A Game for All 14
Making It Big 16
Being a Good Sport 18
A Healthy Game 20
Tetherball Quiz 22
Key Words/Index 23

TETHERBALL 3

BACKYARD GAMES

What Is Tetherball?

Playing backyard games is a fun way to spend leisure time on a warm, sunny day. It gives friends and family of all ages the chance to get together and **socialize**. Playing games can also be a good form of exercise.

One of the simplest and best-known backyard games is tetherball. In this game, a ball is "tethered," or attached, to an upright pole by a cord. The goal of the game is to see who can wrap the cord around the pole first by hitting the ball in one direction.

The history of tetherball dates back to the late 1800s. Originally, the game used a tennis ball, which was hit by **rackets**, not hands. It was a popular backyard game when it was first invented. It was also enjoyed on ships. Today, this form of tetherball, better known as swingball, is popular in United Kingdom and many other countries.

Over time, the game **evolved** into the American form of tetherball. In this version of the game, the ball is similar to a volleyball, and it is hit by hands, not rackets. Tetherball is now played in backyards, schoolyards, and recreation centers across the United States.

Timeline

From children and teens to soldiers and families, playing tetherball has been a source of enjoyment and exercise for many people over the years.

1875–1896
Tetherball is invented in Ireland in 1875. It is played using a tennis ball and rackets.

1897
British tetherball is promoted in the United States. People like the game because it can be played in a small space.

1943
Tetherball is a popular game played by U.S. Army soldiers in World War II. If soldiers do not have a tennis ball, they use a volleyball and hit it with their hands.

BACKYARD GAMES

Approximately 80 players compete in San Diego's first tetherball tournament, in California.

Tim Ingram starts the World Tetherball Association. Approximately 1,000 people participate in an event called the World Tetherball Championships in Palm Springs, California.

2007

2011

2020

The COVID pandemic causes a spike in the purchases of tetherball sets as people try to stay active during lockdowns.

What You Need

Tetherball does not require very much equipment. The only essentials are a pole, cord, ball, and base. A tetherball set, which includes all of these items, is available at many stores and is fairly inexpensive.

Optional tetherball equipment may include a hand pump for the ball, a **pole sleeve**, and a score sheet. These can also be found online.

Keeping the ball fully pumped means that it will be bouncy and respond well to each hit from the players.

BACKYARD GAMES

Cord
The cord connecting the ball to the pole is usually made of heavy-duty nylon. It should be 2 feet (0.6 m) shorter than the pole.

Base
Poles are often secured to the ground with a cement base. Sometimes, a base is sold as part of a tetherball kit. It is often made of metal or hard plastic. Hollow bases can be weighted down with water or sand.

Pole
A tetherball pole needs to be sturdy. Many are made of steel for this reason. The pole is between 7 and 10 feet (2 and 3 meters) in height. Often, it comes in several pieces which are easy to put together.

Ball
A tetherball is 25 to 27 inches (65 to 67 centimeters) in **circumference** and weighs 9 to 10 ounces (260 to 280 grams). The ball is covered with a padded material. It has a rope attached to it.

TETHERBALL

The Court

Tetherball games take place on a playing field called a **court**. The court is a circle that is about 20 feet (6 m) in **diameter**. The tetherball pole is placed in the center of this circle. This is divided into four parts. Two sections are playing zones, and the other two are **neutral** zones.

The players face each other in the playing zones. The neutral zones separate the two playing zones. Players can decide if they want to use the neutral zones as a playing area or not. If they decide that it is out-of-bounds, then stepping into a neutral zone counts as a foul.

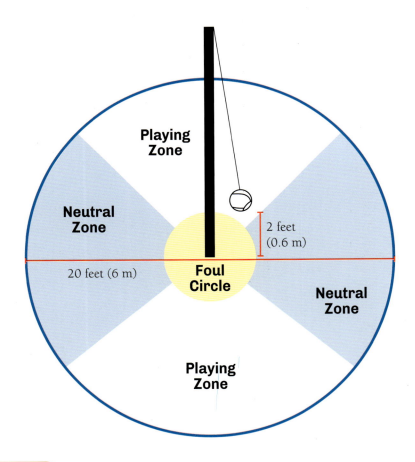

A foul circle that is 6 feet (1.8 m) in diameter surrounds the tetherball pole. No player is allowed to step inside this area. There is also a foul mark on the tetherball pole at the 5-foot (1.5 m) mark.

The tetherball should hang 2 feet (0.6 m) from the ground no matter how high the pole.

The court should be level with no obstacles that a player could stumble over. Tetherball may be played on a variety of surfaces, including concrete, sand, gravel, and grass.

Tetherball courts are located in all kinds of public places, including beaches.

TETHERBALL 11

Rules of the Game

Tetherball is usually played by two people. Each player stays on his or her half of the court. Since tetherball is not an official sport, rules for the game vary. The goal of the game is to wrap the cord around the pole in the player's direction so that the ball cannot be wrapped further and rests against the pole.

Taking Turns

The players decide who will **serve** first, and afterwards they alternate. The server selects the direction of the ball.

Serve

The player who is serving pulls the ball away from the pole, throws it up in the air, and hits it toward the receiver. The other player will try to hit the ball in the opposite direction.

Fouls

Players may not catch, throw, or hold the ball. They may not cross over to the other player's side of the court. They are not allowed to hit the ball with anything but their hands or arms. A player loses the game if he or she commits three fouls.

Keeping Score

The first player to wrap the pole wins the game. A match can be made up of seven games. The winner is the one who wins the most games.

A Game for All

Tetherball is an easy game to learn and is fun to play. It can be played almost anywhere. If players do not have a pole, they can tether the ball to a suitable tree.

Tetherball can be played by people of varying ages and skill levels. Tetherball poles come in different sizes. This allows children as well as adults to play the game.

Most people play casual games of tetherball. Besides backyards, this game is popular wherever there is a level space and somewhere to hang the tetherball.

Some families make tetherball part of an active summer day.

BACKYARD GAMES

People can often be seen playing tetherball in playgrounds, parks, summer camps, and aboard ships. Often, community organizations will host a tetherball contest or tournament. These contests and tournaments are divided into groups based on age. There are tournaments for children and adults.

Playing tetherball can help to build a sense of community.

Also Known As!

Tetherball has been known by at least **four** names, including **bumble-puppy**.

Flashback!

Peter Cow introduced an early version of **tetherball**, more than **100** years ago. It was called **spiropole**.

Making It Big

Tetherball is a popular activity, but it is not considered a **professional sport**. Nevertheless, many organizations, including summer camps and businesses, regularly host or sponsor informal tournaments.

Many people wish tetherball was a professional sport. The National Tetherball League was formed in 2009 and continued until 2016. In 2011, the World Tetherball Association was created. It held the first and only World Tetherball **Championships** in the same year.

Tetherball can be a very competitive game, with players working hard for the win.

Tim Ingram

Tim was a professional hockey and soccer player as a young man. He moved from Canada to Desert Hot Springs in California. In 2008, he founded the Camp of Champions, which provides free sports programs for local youth.

One game his own children enjoyed was tetherball. This led Tim to create the World Tetherball Association in 2011. That year, the association hosted the first ever three-day World Tetherball Championships. The event was held at Knott's Soak City, in Palm Springs, California. About 1,000 people participated, including 160 schoolchildren.

Being a Good Sport

Tetherball games can be fun, but it is important to be a good sport and follow the rules. The rules help prevent injury and ensure everyone has a good time. In 2010 alone, more 1,000 injuries were caused by a tetherball.

Following some simple rules can keep players and spectators safe. Before a game, players should check that the pole is firmly in the ground or its base, and that the tetherball is securely attached to the pole. They should also make sure the court is ready and remove any obstacles.

Standing back and staying quiet when others are playing shows respect.

BACKYARD GAMES

Players should point out the court boundaries to any people watching. Spectators are not allowed on the court when a game is in progress. This prevents them from being hit by a flying ball.

Players need to be alert as they play. They must stay in their playing area, unless it has been agreed they can play in the neutral area also. No one should distract or disturb the players when the game is in progress.

As the ball unwraps from the pole, the playing area will get larger. It is important to always make sure there is enough room to play.

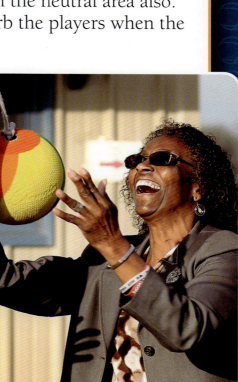

Tetherball can be great fun as long as the players stick to the rules.

A Healthy Game

Tetherball is a great way for people to increase their fitness. The game can be tiring because it involves running, jumping, and hitting. This helps build players' arm and leg muscles.

Tetherball helps players develop **stamina**, agility, and flexibility. It is also a great way to improve hand-eye coordination. Better health has benefits in all areas of life, not just in sport.

An individual can use a tetherball set to have a fun workout.

Tetherball keeps players' bodies in constant motion.

Tetherball may also strengthen a player's mental health. The physical activity helps players relax and may reduce their anxiety. They will also receive fresh air and sunshine, which lifts mood.

People who play tetherball can often learn patience and **strategic** planning skills as they play. They will also learn relationship skills as they interact with other players and spectators.

Attention!
Playing tetherball, and other outdoor games, for **20 minutes a day**, helps kids stay focused in school.

Light Power!
Playing outdoors in the sunlight boosts **vitamin D** levels. Vitamin D **strengthens** players' **bones**.

Tetherball Quiz

1 What type of ball was used when tetherball was first invented?

2 Why did people like tetherball when it was first developed?

3 What did some soldiers use as a tetherball in World War II?

4 What four pieces of equipment are needed to play tetherball?

5 How high is a tetherball pole?

6 What should be cleared from the court before each game?

7 How many fouls can a player commit before forfeiting the game?

8 Besides backyards, where is tetherball played?

ANSWERS
1 A tennis ball **2** It could be played in a small space. **3** A volleyball **4** A pole, cord, ball, and base **5** 7 to 10 feet (2 to 3 m) **6** Obstacles **7** Three **8** Playgrounds, schoolyards, ships, recreation centers, parks, and summer camps

22 BACKYARD GAMES

Key Words

championships: contests to determine the best or winning player or team

circumference: the distance around the edge of a circle

court: an area where a game is played

diameter: the distance from one point on a circle through the center to another point on the circle

evolved: developed from one form to another

neutral: not belonging or supporting ether side

pole sleeve: a part placed in the ground that holds the pole during play and allows the pole to be removed when not in use

professional sport: sports in which participants are paid money

rackets: paddles with netting stretched across the frame above the handle

serve: hitting the ball

socialize: spending time relaxing with friends

stamina: being fit and having the ability to keep being active

strategic: something done in order to achieve some specific goal

Index

ball 5, 6, 8, 9, 12, 13, 14, 18, 19, 22

base 8, 9, 18, 22

cord 5, 8, 9, 12, 22

court 10, 11, 12, 13, 18, 22

Cow, Peter 15

equipment 8, 9, 22

exercise 5, 6, 20, 21

foul 10, 11, 13, 22

health 20, 21

Ingram, Tim 7, 17

National Tetherball League 16

playing area 10, 19

pole 5, 8, 9, 10, 11, 12, 13, 14, 18, 22

rules 12, 18, 19

score 8, 13

swingball 5

World Tetherball Association 7, 16, 17

World Tetherball Championships 7, 16, 17

Get the best of both worlds.

AV2 bridges the gap between print and digital.

The expandable resources toolbar enables quick access to content including **videos**, **audio**, **activities**, **weblinks**, **slideshows**, **quizzes**, and **key words**.

Animated videos make static images come alive.

Resource icons on each page help readers to further **explore key concepts**.

Published by Lightbox Learning
276 5th Avenue, Suite 704 #917
New York, NY 10001
Website: www.openlightbox.com

Copyright ©2022 Lightbox Learning
All rights reserved. No part of this publication may be reproduced, stored in a retrieval system, or transmitted in any form or by any means, electronic, mechanical, photocopying, recording, or otherwise, without the prior written permission of the publisher.

Library of Congress Cataloging-in-Publication Data
Names: Coupé, Jessica, author.
Title: Tetherball / Jessica Coupé.
Description: New York, NY : AV2, 2022. | Series: Backyard games | Includes index. | Audience: Grades 2-3
Identifiers: LCCN 2021030400 (print) | LCCN 2021030401 (ebook) | ISBN 9781791142179 (library binding) | ISBN 9781791142186 (paperback) | ISBN 9781791142193
Subjects: LCSH: Tetherball--Juvenile literature.
Classification: LCC GV1017.T47 C68 2022 (print) | LCC GV1017.T47 (ebook) | DDC 796.31--dc23
LC record available at https://lccn.loc.gov/2021030400
LC ebook record available at https://lccn.loc.gov/2021030401

Printed in Guangzhou, China
1 2 3 4 5 6 7 8 9 0 25 24 23 22 21

082021
101120

Project Coordinator Heather Kissock
Designer Terry Paulhus

Photo Credits
Every reasonable effort has been made to trace ownership and to obtain permission to reprint copyright material. The publisher would be pleased to have any errors or omissions brought to its attention so that they may be corrected in subsequent printings. AV2 acknowledges Getty Images, Alamy, Shutterstock, and Dreamstime as its primary photo suppliers for this title.